TRUTH

AND

LOVE

The Timeless Message of 1–3 John

ISBN 978-1-0877-6733-8
Item 005838138
Dewey Decimal Classification Number: 242
Subject Heading: DEVOTIONAL LITERATURE / BIBLE STUDY AND TEACHING / GOD

Printed in the United States of America

Student Ministry Publishing
Lifeway Resources
One Lifeway Plaza
Nashville, Tennessee 37234

We believe that the Bible has God for its author; salvation for its end; and truth, without any mixture of error, for its matter and that all Scripture is totally true and trustworthy. To review Lifeway's doctrinal guideline, please visit www.lifeway.com/doctrinalguideline.

PUBLISHING TEAM

Director, Student Ministry
Ben Trueblood

Manager, Student Ministry Publishing
John Paul Basham

Editorial Team Leader
Karen Daniel

Writer
Stephanie Cross

Content Editor
Kyle Wiltshire

Production Editor
April-Lyn Caouette

Graphic Designer
Shiloh Stufflebeam

TABLE OF CONTENTS

INTRO

As humans, we often try to overcomplicate things. Have you ever gotten directions like: "At the stop sign, you'll see a tree that got struck by lightning in 2014 and that my brother once fell out of when he was eight. My grandfather planted that tree the day he asked my grandmother to marry him. Anyway, turn right there"? A simple "turn right at the stop sign" would have sufficed. Isn't it refreshing when someone keeps it simple?

Two simple words characterize all three of John's letters: *truth* and *love*. Written by the apostle John (who was known as "the beloved disciple" and "the one Jesus loved"), these letters overflow with instructions to "love God" and "love one another." We know Jesus said these were the two greatest commands, so it's no surprise that John, one of His closest friends, would focus on these essential truths to love, lead, comfort, and encourage the early church—especially since false teachers were popping up all over and the people had questions. John provided clear answers.

John's heartfelt invitation cries to his readers, "Come on, let's just get back to the basics." He wanted to help people know the truth of the gospel. Knowing the truth leads us to a love greater than we've ever known and causes us to love others more than we ever thought possible.

Over the next thirty days, we'll get to the heart of John's message and answer these three essential questions as we go:

What do John's letters teach us about God/Jesus?

What do John's letters teach us about ourselves and others?

What do John's letters teach us about obeying God's commands and living out the truth?

We're going to try to keep it simple over the next thirty days and focus on nothing but truth and love. Let's go!

GETTING STARTED

*This devotional contains thirty days of content, broken down into sections. Each day is divided into three elements—**discover, delight,** and **display**—to help you grow in your faith.*

discover

This section helps you examine the passage in light of who God is and determine what it says about your identity in relationship to Him. Included here is the daily Scripture reading and key verses, along with illustrations and commentary to guide you as you learn more about God's Word.

delight

In this section, you'll be challenged by questions and activities that help you see how God is alive and active in every detail of His Word and your life.

display

Here's where you take action. This section calls you to apply what you've learned through each day.

Each day also includes a prayer activity at the conclusion of the devotion.

Throughout the devotional, you'll also find extra items to help you connect with the topic personally, such as Scripture memory verses, additional resources, and interactive articles.

Truth and Love

1 JOHN

SECTION 1

Even the early church had haters. Some never believed to begin with (Roman persecutors), while others deviated from the truth of the gospel message (false teachers). It's likely that by this time, the Romans had already destroyed the temple and wrecked the Holy City of Jerusalem.

From his new home in Ephesus, John wrote a letter of reassurance and reminder to new Christians, reminding them that they were saved by faith in Jesus, who was exactly who He claimed to be. In response, they were to obey God's commands: love God with all their heart, and love others well. John's call has reverberated through the years to us today.

TRUTH AFFIRMED

discover

READ 1 JOHN 1:1-4.

**What was from the beginning, what we have heard, what we
have seen with our eyes, what we have observed and have
touched with our hands, concerning the word of life . . .
— 1 John 1:1**

Have you ever played a game called "Telephone"? One person shares a
short message with the next, and that person attempts to pass it on exactly
as they heard it. This keeps going until the last person shares what they
heard. Usually, the final message is a far cry from the original. Messages
tend to get twisted as they become interpretations, passed from person to
person over time.

John saw this happening as false teachers rose up and gave their opinions
about who Jesus was and what that meant. They were distorting the
message. But John had been there. He had lived life with Jesus. He had
heard Jesus speak the truth. He had seen Jesus live it out. He had walked
and talked and ate with Jesus. And he had even "leaned back against
Jesus" (John 13:25) as Jesus explained that one of His closest friends would
betray Him.

Through John's own story, Jesus's very real presence and ministry was
affirmed: the same Jesus, who was from the beginning and is forever, walked
among them in the flesh. Not only was that truth affirmed to believers in
John's day, but through his story, the truth is affirmed to us today, as well.

delight

Describe a time when what you were told happened and what actually happened were very different realities.

What was "revealed to" the apostles? How? Explain.

display

People needed God to help them see the truth, and He did so by sending and revealing Jesus. Through the Holy Spirit, God inspired those who walked with Jesus (like John) to "testify" (give evidence) about what they saw, heard, and touched. Through their testimony, we, who still need to see the truth, hear the gospel message.

Think about what your earliest encounters with the gospel message were like. What are ways you have seen, heard, and touched the gospel message? Write about them below.

Father, help me to see the truth about who Jesus is and what it means that You sent Him to save us. Show me how I can "testify" about the truth to people around me, and help me to be bold enough to do it.

DARKNESS UNDONE

discover

READ 1 JOHN 1:5-9.

**This is the message we have heard from him and declare to you: God is light, and there is absolutely no darkness in him.
—1 John 1:5**

If you've ever walked out of a dark movie theater and into a sunny day, you know how painful it can be as your eyes adjust. Our eyes get used to the darkness gradually, but it takes only seconds for the light to undo what the darkness has done.[1] Moving from a dark room into bright light shocks our eyes into a protective filtering mode so we can see rightly.

John leaves no room for disagreement: God is light. This is His true nature. The good news for us is that Jesus, being one with the Father (see John 10:30), is also light. When we confess our sins and put our faith in Him for salvation, Paul said we're "alive to God in Christ Jesus" (Rom. 6:11). Thus, if we are in Him, we are in the light, and there's no room for darkness in us, either.

Moving from spiritual darkness to light isn't easy—it's a complete shock to our system. But the shift is immediate. Our spiritual eyes adjust to the light as we step out of the darkness of sin and into the glorious, eternal light of Christ (see Rev. 21:23-24). By His light we can see the way to live a God-honoring life.

delight

Since God is light, He sees us clearly. What are some ways you try to hide things from God?

What does the image of God as light say to you about His character? Where else in Scripture do you see this imagery?

display

"Confessing our sins does not mean a shallow reciting of misdeeds."[2] Moving from darkness to light means nothing is hidden—even the stuff we wish would remain unknown. But God won't shame you or tell everyone what you've done. Jesus took the shame of your sin on Himself at the cross; there's no shame or fear when confessing to God. He loves us with a perfect love that runs deeper than we'll ever know.

Ask the Holy Spirit to guide you as you examine your heart. Whatever remains in darkness in your life, confess it to God. Forgiveness awaits (see 1 John 1:9).

God, I know I've sinned. But I also know that because of who You are, I don't have to be afraid. I can confess and be forgiven. Please help me to honor You by walking in the light and seeking forgiveness for moments when I fail.

HONOR, NOT SHAME

discover

READ 1 JOHN 2:1-2.

He himself is the atoning sacrifice for our sins, and not only for ours, but also for those of the whole world.
—1 John 2:2

When we recognize our sin and step out of darkness into light, we might still be tempted to feel shame for what we've done in the past. Or maybe we're still in the darkness, feeling too ashamed to take that first step into the light. This has happened from the very first time sin entered the world—God came looking for Adam and Eve, just like Jesus came for you, and they hid. Maybe you've found yourself wanting to do the same?

While this is a natural, human reaction to our mistakes, it shows that we don't fully understand what Jesus has done for us. Jesus is our advocate and our substitute. On the cross, Jesus was bruised, broken, bloody, abandoned by His friends, mocked by the world—and in His darkest moment, heard nothing but silence from His Father (see Matt. 27:46).

To die on the cross was considered a curse, but Jesus "endured . . . despising the shame" (Heb. 12:2) of the cross to break the curse of sin and death over us. When Jesus said, "It is finished" (John 19:30), He was speaking to shame then, too. Now, He is seated in the place of honor by the Father's right hand. And while He's there, He's not looking down on us—He's lifting our heads with an invitation: *Come, follow Me.*

delight

When you feel ashamed of something you've done, what's your natural response? What would it take for you to bring your shame to Jesus instead?

What does Jesus's path from the cross to God's right hand reveal to you about His love?

display

"God's justice demands satisfaction. God's love provided that."[3] Some people view God's demand of satisfaction for sin as harsh. But the truth is, God did the work by providing everything we would need to satisfy Him in Jesus. We don't carry the weight—Jesus does. This is His incredible kindness to us. He calls us to give this same kindness to others, no matter what they've done to us.

Name some people you know who don't know Jesus. Then write out one way you can show them kindness.

Father, thank You for loving me when I was difficult to love. Thank You for sending Jesus to pay for my sins and restore my relationship with You. Help me to love others even when they don't make it easy.

KNOWING HIM

discover

READ 1 JOHN 2:3-6.

This is how we know that we know him: if we keep his commands.
—1 John 2:3

Think about a rule that isn't always easy to follow. Maybe all your homework has to be done before you can hang out with your friends. Maybe you have to do the dishes on Thursdays before you can watch Netflix. Maybe you have to make a certain grade to go on the field trip or be done with an assignment at a certain time to attend the pep rally. You might say you follow the rule to avoid punishment or to be allowed to do something fun, but ultimately, you're respecting the rule-maker's authority in your life. You're showing honor and even love.

Although Jesus obeyed every one of God's commands perfectly, He knows what this obedience—even to difficult commands—is like. He will never ask us to do something He isn't willing to do Himself. He knew God's plan included the cross, asked if there was another way, then reaffirmed that He was absolutely committed to do God's will (see Luke 22:42). In His own words, "[S]o that the world may know that I love the Father, I do as the Father commanded me" (John 14:31).

The simplest way to look at it is this: if we belong to God, we'll act like it. We'll follow Jesus's example and obey His commands "so that the world may know" we love God.

delight

Which of God's commands are most difficult for you to follow? Which are the easiest? Why?

What does your attitude toward God's commands say about your heart toward Him? Explain.

display

Only Jesus could obey God perfectly. But God has given us an incredible gift in the Holy Spirit who "will teach you all things and remind you of everything" Jesus taught (John 14:26), including God's love for us (see Rom. 5:5). Put simply: the Holy Spirit empowers us to follow God's will for our lives. We align our hearts with God's will by spending time with Him, and the two main ways we do this are Bible study and prayer.

In your prayer time today, or as a journaled prayer below, ask the Holy Spirit to help you understand and apply what you've read today.

Jesus, thank You. Thank You for not only making a way for me to have a relationship with God, but also for showing me the right way to grow it. Help me to obey even the commands that are most difficult for me.

MEMORY
VERSE

He himself is the atoning sacrifice for our sins, and not only for ours, but also for those of the whole world.

—1 John 2:2

BROTHERS & SISTERS

discover

READ 1 JOHN 2:7-11.

But the one who hates his brother or sister is in the darkness, walks in the darkness, and doesn't know where he's going, because the darkness has blinded his eyes.
—1 John 2:11

When Jesus calls you to walk in the light, He doesn't say, "Okay, now that you're in the light, My job is done." Rather, He says, "Okay, now that you're in the light, here's how you can *keep* walking in the light." Though we probably won't hear His voice audibly, we know how to walk in the light because of God's Word. According to Jesus, the most important command is to love God with all that we are and the second most important is to love others (see Matt. 22:37-40).

John wrote a lot about love, too. In fact, John greeted his readers with the phrase "Dear Friends," which means "beloved" or "worthy of love." In doing this, not only was John expressing his own love for the readers, but he was also pointing them back to the One who first called us beloved (see 1 John 4:19). This term is used over and over to describe Jesus as well as the "children of God" (John 1:12)—our brothers and sisters "in Christ" (see Rom. 6:11).

Loving your brothers and sisters in Christ—no matter if they annoy you or have hurt you in the past—is part of being in the light. Jesus loved us even when we were against Him, and we should love others the same way.

delight

Let's take Jesus at face value. What are ways that hating others hurts you in the long run?

Have you ever been blinded by hatred? How does love overcome hatred and create heart change?

display

God is love, and hate is everything that God is not. Hate is:

Short-tempered	Unforgiving	Wishy-washy
Unkind	Chaotic	Bad
Powerless	Temporary	Unholy
Unjust	Spiteful	Vengeful
Ignorant	Negative	

Highlight or circle any words that stand out to you on this list. Explain why, and then describe how love—and God—is the opposite. If you find any of these characteristics in your own life, confess them to God and ask Him to help you live out love.

Lord, help me love my brothers and sisters in Christ, no matter what. Help me to be an example for those who don't know You. Let Your love show to the world through our love for one another.

CONQUERED

discover

READ 1 JOHN 2:12-14.

I have written to you, children, because you have come to know the Father. I have written to you, fathers, because you have come to know the one who is from the beginning. I have written to you, young men, because you are strong, God's word remains in you, and you have conquered the evil one.
—1 John 2:14

There are many ways you could choose to remember something: you might write it down, set a reminder on your phone, leave a sticky note where you know you'll see it, or tell someone else, "Remind me . . ." But have you ever noticed the difference between trying to remember a fact and trying to remember a feeling? Maybe our hearts forget quicker than our brains, and they, too, must be reminded of what's true.

Knowing how forgetful our hearts are, John wrote to his friends to remind them that the evil one had already been conquered by Jesus— and in Him, we have victory. No matter how the enemy attacks or tempts or comes after us, no matter how many times you doubt or struggle, and no matter how often you fall into sin, you are still forgiven. In Jesus, your place of belonging is victory, and that isn't something that can be taken from you (see John 10:28-30). So no matter how often you need to do it, remind yourself of this: in Christ, the evil one is already conquered.

delight

List the different messages John gave to each group.

    Children:

    Fathers:

    Young Men:

Why do you think John had different messages for each group? Which message speaks to you most?

display

We all need a reminder from time to time that Jesus has conquered the evil one, our enemy. Through His grace, we receive forgiveness that lasts forever; nothing the enemy does to us or in the world will change that. Sometimes we forget this when we mess up or when the world is locked in chaos. Here are some ideas of ways to remind yourself and others of this truth:

Stay in Scripture. Keep praying. Tell others about what you're going through—and invite them to do the same, helping bear their burden and meeting them where they are in their struggle. Describe ways you see God working in your life.

How else could you remind yourself and others that through Jesus's work on the cross, we are forgiven forever? List some more ideas below.

Father, when I become busy, or mess up, or feel like the world has gone crazy, sometimes I forget that I'm forgiven and that Jesus has already conquered the enemy. No matter what's going on in my life or in the world, help me to remember Jesus and have peace.

FOREVER

discover

READ 1 JOHN 2:15-17.

**And the world with its lust is passing away, but the
one who does the will of God remains forever.
—1 John 2:17**

Have you collected some favorite t-shirts over the years? Maybe you
still have your first soccer jersey, or a shirt from the first concert you ever
attended or a student ministry event. If you have a collection of old t-shirts,
there are likely some that you just can't wear anymore; you've outgrown
them or they're just too ratty and faded to wear. Sure, you could have them
made into a blanket, but eventually, that will become tattered and frayed,
as well.

Everything in this world has a lifespan, from our t-shirts to our days at school
right down to our bodies. While our souls are eternal, our bodies and the
things we own—and even some of the things we love to do—are not. While
this might sound a little depressing, the good news is that evil's reign in the
world is also subject to a lifespan.

Jesus has already defeated sin and death, but we still live in a world very
much affected by both. One day, that won't be the case. One day, Jesus will
return. One day, He will establish a new heaven and earth, and the world as
we know it—the things we enjoy as well as the things we hate—will be gone.
Our souls, though, live on—either in the presence of God or separated
from Him. For the believer, the "one who does the will of God," this is good
news: we "remain" with Him forever.

delight

What are some things you love that you might need to let go of?

What are some things you need to embrace that are eternal?

display

John described the world by using the word "lust"—a deep desire for something that doesn't belong to us. Lust can be of the flesh, the eyes, or even our pride. As Bede pointed out, "These few words describe every kind of wickedness which exists."[4] We can't love the evil of the world and be pursuing God's restorative purpose for it at the same time. To love the lost in the world, we must live in a way that might seem strange.

Prayerfully consider your life, then list out three habits to break, two changes to make, and one risk to take to honor God.

Three habits to break:

Two changes to make:

One risk to take:

God, sometimes it's easy to get caught up in what I want, what I have, or what I don't have. Forgive me for the times I've put the things I own and enjoy above You or pursued them instead of Your kingdom. Help me live with a focus on the right things.

NO LIE

discover

READ 1 JOHN 2:18-23.

I have not written to you because you don't know the truth, but because you do know it, and no lie comes from the truth.
—1 John 2:21

Think about how many "voices" speak into your life daily—the authority figures in your home or at school, the people you follow on social media, the news app on your phone, and even your friends or acquaintances. While many of the voices closest to you are likely trustworthy and help you determine what's true, it can be difficult to know exactly who to trust or what to believe.

When John wrote these letters, the church was new, still learning and growing in the gospel. But at the same time, false teachers were telling them that Jesus wasn't the Messiah and that God didn't really come in the flesh. John wasn't teaching the readers anything new by telling them Jesus was the Messiah; he was reminding them of what they already knew.

Here's the thing: God can't lie. It's just not in His character. Jesus is one with God the Father, so Jesus can't lie, either. Both proclaimed the truth that Jesus is the Messiah—that Jesus came to earth, lived a perfect life, died for our sins, and rose to life, defeating sin and death. When we know God, we know truth. When we know the truth, we can easily identify the lies. Because nothing that comes from God can be a lie, we can trust what He says. And we can know what He says by studying His Word and praying.

delight

When is it tough for you to remember the truth about Jesus?

How does it comfort you to know that God can't lie and that everything that comes from Him is true?

display

There are two other key words in this passage that help us with remembering what we know to be true from God's Word: "anointing" (v. 20) and "confess[ing]" (v. 23). Anointing is something the Spirit does, not us; this happens when we trust in Jesus for salvation. Confessing is something we do with our words and our lives.

If you haven't trusted Jesus as Savior, talk with a trusted adult about doing so. If you have, thank Him for that gift.

List some ways you can "confess" the truth about Jesus with your words and actions this month:

Thank You, God, for giving us Jesus to forgive our sins. Thank You for giving us the Holy Spirit and Your Word to help us know truth, as well. I know I can trust You; lying isn't compatible with Your nature. Help me to easily see when people are lying about You.

REMAIN

discover

READ 1 JOHN 2:24-29.

I have written these things to you concerning those who are trying to deceive you.
—1 John 2:26

Repeated words are important words, and in these six verses alone, we see some form of the word "remain" six times. According to John:

- What we have heard from the beginning remains (v. 24).

- We remain in the Son and the Father (v. 24).

- Our anointing (the Holy Spirit) remains in us (v. 27).

- We are commanded to remain in Christ (v. 27).

Today, *remain* can mean "stay with me," "don't change," or "you won't be destroyed." However, the original Greek word that John used in these verses means "to continue." Now, this isn't saying we have to continue something to keep our salvation; rather, when we continue in obedience to God's Word, we show evidence of our salvation. This evidence is given to us by God.

Essentially, the promise for those who remain is that Christ remains in us—in other words, we gain eternal life. When people try to get us to doubt Jesus— and they will—that can lead us to doubt these promises, too. However, the truth remains the truth, no matter what people say. So, we trust in God. We trust that Jesus is who He says He is and did what the Bible said He did. And we trust that the Holy Spirit seals us with this promise for salvation and eternal life.

delight

According to this passage, how can you know God will keep all of His promises?

What does "remaining" do for us?

Truth and Love

display

We've already talked about shame, and we know it's not something God wants for us: John says that we should "remain in him so that when he appears, we may have confidence and not be ashamed before him at his coming" (v. 28). People might say things about your faith that make you feel wrong or unintelligent, but you're not. You know the truth! So have confidence and stand firm in Jesus, knowing that your reward for trusting in Him is eternal life with Him.

Think about something someone might say you're wrong about or put you down for believing. List a few God-honoring ways that you could respond if that situation ever arose.

Father, forgive me for the times when I've backed down or stayed quiet because of what others say about You. Help me to love them as You have called me to, while also not compromising my faith. I pray that I would always trust that what Your Word says is true.

WONDER & AWE

discover

READ 1 JOHN 3:1-3.

Dear friends, we are God's children now, and what we will be has not yet been revealed. We know that when He appears, we will be like him because we will see him as he is.
—1 John 3:2

How often do you say, "That's awesome" or "That's amazing" to describe an everyday occurrence or product? Or to describe a stunning view? Though this last usage would be more in line with the true definition, it still falls short. To be *in awe* ("awe-some") or *amazed* ("amazing") indicates that you view something with childlike wonder or complete surprise; these words carry a deeper meaning than we often assign to them.

The same is true of John's words in verse 1, "what great love the Father has given us." John was expressing a sense of wonder, admiration, and astonishment at the idea that God loves us so much that He calls us His children. We see this feeling conveyed in the next two verses as well: it's amazing that we'll have the hope of seeing Jesus as He is when He returns, and that we will be like Him—not in His nature as God, but in holiness and physically in our resurrected bodies.

Because of this promise that God will complete the good work He began in us (see Phil. 1:6), we look to Jesus now, too. We see Him as we're able through the Bible and the Holy Spirit, and through that, we seek to live in line with God's will—and filled with His joy, just as children should be.

delight

What might it be like for you to view God's love with childlike wonder, awe, or amazement?

How does the hope of seeing Jesus and becoming like Him encourage you to live today?

display

The "hope" John mentioned in verse 3 also has a deeper meaning than what we might think. It's a hope in three things: Jesus's return, our seeing Him, and our being made like Him. It's also "a confident expectation of the future, a trust in God's provision, and the patience of waiting for him."[5]

Write out a few ideas of how you might live . . .

. . . with expectation of the future:

. . . trusting God's provision:

. . . patiently waiting for Him:

Jesus, thank You for going before me in every way—showing me how to live and giving me eternal life through Your own resurrection. Help me to live in light of this hope each day and to call others' attention to that hope, too.

COVERED

discover

READ 1 JOHN 3:4-10.

**You know that he was revealed so that he might
take away sins, and there is no sin in him.**
—1 John 3:5

In 1999, Tony Hawk did something most people thought was impossible:
he landed the world's first 900. A 900 is a spin with two and a half rotations
performed while skateboarding off of a ramp. It was an epic moment!
Now, anyone who jumps on a skateboard and tries to do a 900 is merely
mimicking Tony Hawk. In a weird way, this idea mirrors our relationship with
Jesus. He did what no one else had ever done before—He lived a perfectly
righteous life. Where Jesus and Tony's accomplishments differ is that many
folks have now completed a 900 since Tony performed that first one—but no
one will ever do what Jesus did again.

John used strong language here, calling sin "lawlessness" and saying
those who sin are "of the devil," while those who remain in Jesus don't sin.
At first glance, this might seem like John was saying we would never sin
again. But that's not what he meant. He meant that those who continue in
righteousness give evidence of their faith by not practicing perpetual and
habitual sin in their life.

Because we are by nature lawless, sinful people, we couldn't possibly ever
follow God's law perfectly. You can pursue good but not be entirely free of
sin. Jesus is not lawless; He is good and free of sin. He did what we never
could in His life: He established our righteousness by covering us with His in
His death and resurrection.

delight

What did John say about those who do what's right? What about those who don't? Explain.

How does it give you confidence and comfort to know that Jesus's perfect righteousness covers your sin when you trust Him for salvation? How does this inspire you to live?

display

A Christ follower's pattern should be in pursuit of Jesus. Jesus transforms us as we pursue Him in this process called *sanctification*, the Spirit's work of making us holy and empowering us to live out our new life in Christ.

List one specific way you can pursue holiness this week. (Think: What step of obedience is God calling me to take?)

Write out your commitment to pursuing holiness as a pattern of life. Consider writing this as a prayer, using the prompt at the bottom of the page to guide you.

Father, forgive me for the times I choose sin over obeying You. Please help me see how each choice leads to righteousness or lawlessness and to obey the Holy Spirit's leading as I make those choices. Guide me to model my life's pattern after Jesus's, to willingly obey You.

PROVEN

discover

READ 1 JOHN 3:11-18.

**Little children, let us not love in word or
speech, but in action and in truth.**
—1 John 3:18

Have you ever been guilty of bragging about something you weren't
really that good at then been proven wrong? For instance, saying
you could dunk a basketball and only being able to jump a foot off
the ground? Or claiming you could hit high notes like Ariana Grande
but knowing your register was actually much lower? Or maybe you've
said something mean about or to a friend in a moment of anger or
misunderstanding. Whatever it was, your actions just didn't line up with
your claims, and you might have been left wondering, "Why did I say
that?" Our claims can be proved right or wrong based on our actions.

When it comes to your faith, you'll probably have "why did I say that?"
moments, too. Since God's work in us is not yet complete (see Phil.
1:6), we will still mess up. But the Holy Spirit's work will be evident in our
lives if we truly are in Christ. Authentic faith, like the kind John spoke
about in these verses, isn't about being perfect or never having to ask,
"why did I . . . ?" Authentic faith means that the pattern of our lives is
arranged in pursuit of Christ. Simply put, what we do and what we say
will share the same message to the people around us: We belong to
Jesus, and He's someone you'll want to follow, too. Come and see.

delight

How do we love in both action and in truth, as John instructed?

Looking at these verses, list some actions that line up with a claim to follow Jesus. What might those look like in your life today?

display

When you live differently, people will notice, and they might not always be nice about it. You could choose to get angry and be hateful right back, but that isn't the kind of response Jesus modeled for us. We can't hold on to both righteousness and sin at the same time. What might you need to let go of so you can hold onto something else?

Use the following word combinations to fill in the blanks below: jealousy/ love; selfishness/service; anxiety/peace; despair/hope; anger/forgiveness. Come up with your own words as you feel led.

"I can let go of _____ to hold on to _____."

You are good and righteous, Jesus—the perfect model for us in everything, including how our words and actions should align with God's will. Thank You for showing me how to love with my words and actions. Help me to respond in love, no matter how people respond to me.

BELIEVE & LOVE

discover

READ 1 JOHN 3:19-24.

Now this is his command: that we believe in the name of his Son, Jesus Christ, and love one another as he commanded us.
—1 John 3:23

Tell the truth on your job application. Show up to school on time. Tell your parents where you're going. Be honest with your friends. These rules might not have major legal ramifications—they might even seem completely random! But they are all important to obey because they serve everyone's best interests. Though disobeying many of God's commands doesn't have legal ramifications, there are still consequences. Both commands in verse 23 serve one ultimate purpose: to show our love to God and to do so by loving one another. This is in everyone's best interest.

While believing in Jesus might seem straightforward, showing that belief through the way we love others might seem daunting. After all, Jesus commanded us to love others as He loves us (see John 13:34)—and His love is perfect (see 1 John 4:18). But in that same verse, we see that Jesus has gone before us in this, too, showing us how to love others through His life and ministry: He lived compassionately. He showed dignity to people no matter who they were. He made time for people and listened to them. He encouraged others. And He constantly called people into the Father's love.

When we trust in Jesus as Savior, we are given the same mission. So, we go, knowing He has gone before us and is with us (see Matt. 28:20).

delight

What do you believe about Jesus, and why does that matter when it comes to loving God and loving others?

John said in verse 24 that one way we know Jesus remains with us is because of the presence of the Holy Spirit in our lives. How do you feel the presence of the Holy Spirit in your life?

display

As Bede said, when we do the work God commands, "we are copying his perfect love to the best of our ability."[6] God alone can truly see what's in our hearts (see 1 Sam. 16:7), but what we do and say flows out of our hearts (see Luke 6:45). So, our desire to do good and love, along with the Holy Spirit's presence, reassures our hearts that we belong to God.

Spend some time in silent prayer, or answer prayerfully in the space below: What do your recent thoughts, words, and actions say about what's in your heart?

Father, thank You for the gift of Your presence in the Holy Spirit. Please shape my heart to look more like Jesus. If I ever experience doubt that I belong to You, remind me of the truth that because Jesus is my Savior, nothing can ever separate me from You.

DEFINED BY TRUTH

discover

READ 1 JOHN 4:1-3.

**Dear friends, do not believe every spirit, but test the
spirits to see if they are from God, because many
false prophets have gone out into the world.**
—1 John 4:1

Throughout his letter, John describes two types of people: those who
are of God and those who are not. Both types are made evident by
what they say and do. Those who are of God are defined by the truth
that Jesus is still working in them and by living out of that truth. Those
who are not of God don't recognize that Jesus is who He claimed to be,
and they live out of that idea.

At the writing of this letter, false teachers were arguing that Jesus didn't
really come to earth in human form, or at the very least, His divine
nature departed from His human one before He went to the cross. They
were taking what God said and twisting it to fulfill their own desires
about the truth of Jesus's identity, the cross, the resurrection, and the
eventual judgment.

God's Word is "from the beginning" (1 John 1:1; see also Gen. 1) and
will never pass away (see Luke 21:33). So, John's call here is to test the
temporary against the eternal. Even the most well-intentioned people
sometimes lie. We must always "test" what we hear against the Word
of God. No matter how good and right something sounds, if it goes
against what God says, it isn't from Him and it isn't true.

John used the term "antichrist" to refer to those who were set against Christ. How do you see evidence today of the "spirit of the antichrist" (v. 3) John mentioned?

When might you be tempted to take someone at their word and not hold it up against Scripture?

display

To test the temporary against the eternal, we must know which is which. When we know God, we can identify the eternal, because all that is eternal comes from Him. We get to know God through prayer and through His Word. Over the next week, write down at least five claims you hear about Jesus—even the ones your pastor or youth pastor make at church. Then, look at Scripture on your own. Next to each claim, note whether Scripture supports it or not. If it does, jot down the reference in the Bible.

Claim	Support

God, so many people claim that their beliefs are true; sometimes it's tough to know what's true and what just sounds good. Please give me wisdom and discernment so I can test the spirits and know what's from You and what isn't.

MEMORY VERSE

Love consists in this:
not that we loved
God, but that he
loved us and sent his
Son to be the atoning
sacrifice for our sins.
—1 John 4:10

COURAGE TO TRY

discover

READ 1 JOHN 4:4-6.

You are from God, little children, and you have conquered them, because the one who is in you is greater than the one who is in the world.
—1 John 4:4

Kids often act as if they're indestructible: leaping from tree houses with blankets as capes, running at full speed until they plop on the floor exhausted, or setting up obstacles to jump with bikes and skateboards. It's possible we carry a bit of this attitude with us throughout life. But the truth is, we're far from indestructible; we're prone to broken arms, scrapes and brusies, and sometimes just needing a good nap. Kids, though, often feel indestructible because they play in the safety of their parents' loving presence. That's the source and secret of their courage to try.

In the same way, God is the Source and Secret to our courage to try; our courage to conquer. Even greater than the courage a kid might gain from the support of a loving parent, God sent Jesus to give us courage by overcoming every obstacle we might face. He is greater than our enemy. He is greater than our biggest challenge. He is greater, period. God has already achieved a victory that we now live in. Knowing God is on our side—that He already sent Jesus to fight evil and sin, and Jesus won—gives us the courage to be "more than conquerors" (Rom. 8:37), no matter what we face.

delight

How does this passage speak to your fears and anxieties?

When have you personally experienced God's greatness?

Describe a time when God helped you "conquer" something that seemed impossible.

display

God is our source for all things. In this passage, John specifically mentioned our victory ("conquered") and truth ("this is how we know the Spirit of truth"). But people who are "from the world" aren't just pulling their beliefs out of thin air: their beliefs are "from the world"—or originating with the "ruler of this world" (John 12:31). What they say tells their origin story, the source of their beliefs.

Write out your own "origin story," describing how your life now points to who your source is. If you feel uncertain, talk about your origin story with your parents, pastor, or youth pastor.

Father, I praise You because You are good—and You are greater than the enemy; You are greater than everyone and everything. Thank You for the victory You have given me in Christ and for the courage You give me through Your Spirit to live in accordance with Your Word and Your will.

REAL LOVE

discover

READ 1 JOHN 4:7-16.

Love consists in this: not that we loved God, but that he loved us and sent his Son to be the atoning sacrifice for our sins.
—1 John 4:10

A common theme in many songs today is doing something—even if you don't want to—because of love. Some of the things done for love in these songs include changing, enduring sorrow, giving up something, persevering when things aren't easy, forgiving, and even taking a certain action or path. While these songs are often talking about love from a secular perspective, we can see all these themes reflected in the Bible, as well.

Here's how Jesus did each of these things because of His love for the Father and us: He came to earth in human form. Even when we were sinners, He endured being mocked, beaten, and hung on a cross. He gave up His divine rights and even His life. He forgave our sin against Him. When the Father didn't provide another way, Jesus stayed on the path that had been set for Him from the beginning.

As Charles Spurgeon said, "It is the greatest marvel that will ever be— that he who is God over all stooped so low as this … that he should bear our sins."[7] This is what real love looks like. This is the gospel— Jesus came and died for our sins. He did it for love.

delight

Read 1 Corinthians 13. List all the characteristics of love given in this passage.

How do those characteristics help you see practical ways to love one another and express God's love to others?

display

While John talked a lot about God's love for us, he also pointed out that "anyone who loves is a child of God and knows God" (1 John 4:7, NLT). We have love ourselves because God gives us His love and the ability to love others comes from that love. When we show love to others, we show that we are of God—His love is "brought to full expression in us" (v. 12, NLT). Because, as John said, "God is love" (v. 16).

This week, note any ways you see God's love for you and any ideas you have for showing love to others.

Jesus, help me know what it means that You "stooped" to bear my sin out of love. Show me how to love others the same way—not looking down on anyone and loving well, no matter who they are. Thank You for Your incredible, relentless love for us.

PERFECT & COMPLETE

discover

READ 1 JOHN 4:17-21.

There is no fear in love; instead, perfect love drives out fear, because fear involves punishment. So the one who fears is not complete in love.
—1 John 4:18

Fear is a common theme today. Maybe you're afraid of heights, snakes, or small spaces. Maybe you're afraid of being alone or of big groups of people. Maybe you're afraid of not accomplishing what you set out to do or of hurting someone. While these fears are certainly valid, they aren't quite the kind of fear John meant. John was talking about the fear of the "day of judgment" (v. 17).

Paul said that "there is now no condemnation for those in Christ Jesus" (Rom. 8:1). When we are "in Christ," we don't have to fear punishment, because His perfect love—so clearly displayed in Jesus's life, death, and resurrection—wipes out our sin debt. We don't "owe" God for our forgiveness; we don't subscribe to God's redemption plan, needing to pay a monthly fee to stay in good standing with Him. Jesus died to pay what we owe, forever. This is what He meant when He said, "It is finished" (John 19:30).

But this doesn't mean we coast through life, living however we want because we know we have forgiveness. This means we live in light of this gift— pursuing Jesus and wholehearted obedience to God's Word. When we do mess up, we don't have to fear that our salvation is gone or that there will be unpaid charges on our account. Jesus's sacrifice—His payment for us—was perfect and complete; it was and always will be enough.

delight

What does it mean to you to know God's love is perfect?

Why is it important to know Jesus's sacrifice on the cross was both perfect and complete?

How might this affect your feelings about the future, specifically the coming judgment?

Truth and Love

display

It can be tough to live as a Christian today, but imagine claiming to be the Messiah in a culture that was even more hostile. Jesus gets it. And yet, though He was in the world, He never feared what was to come, as we sometimes do. He was confident and assured of His Father's love for Him. In a world riddled with anxiety, it's easy for us to slip into fear, but because of Jesus, we don't have to. List some fears you have about the future, then how you can move to confidence and assurance because of God's love for you.

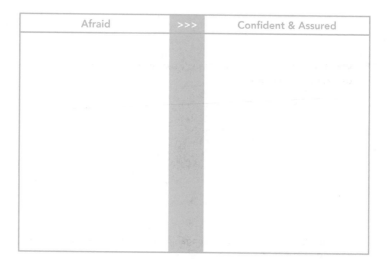

Afraid	>>>	Confident & Assured

Father, thank You for Your perfect love and for sending Your perfect Son to make a way for me to have a relationship with You. Thank You for not leaving any room for fear of what's to come. Help me trust You for the future, even when the present is difficult.

GIFT OF LIFE

discover

READ 1 JOHN 5:1-4.

**For this is what love for God is: to keep his commands.
And his commands are not a burden, because everyone
who has been born of God conquers the world. This is
the victory that has conquered the world: our faith.
—1 John 5:3-4**

When you see the word *love* in John's letters, you might be surprised by the fact that he wasn't talking about his phone, a sport, an idea, or any specific thing. He wasn't even talking about romantic love. If we peeled back the layers covering love's definition, we'd see that words like "strong affection," "admiration," "tenderness," "attachment," and ideas of consistency or kinship are more common.[9] Love, at its root, is people-centered. And according to John, it's God-centered.

Jesus said He came to give us abundant life (see John 10:10). We know that this is a gift of love, as He laid down His life for us (see John 15:13; see also John 10:17-18). This is His love for us. John said if we love God, "we keep His commands" (1 John 3:4). Sometimes, what God asks us to do seems difficult, but our obedience pleases Him—even when it isn't easy. This is our love for Him.

But because God's love is so much greater than we can understand, He offered His Son to carry the weight of our brokenness and make our obedience possible; this is our victory through faith in Him. Jesus carrying our weight doesn't demands our perfection, but His. Through faith in Him, we have the ability to obey Him.

delight

What does it mean that our faith is "the victory"? How does this encourage you toward obedience?

List some ways that you've seen obedience to God lead to abundant life, both in Scripture and in the lives of people you know.

display

Christians will show right belief rather than following false doctrine: we obey God, we resist giving in to selfish desires, and we give love, not hate. When we love others—including God—we'll naturally want to do things that make them happy and bring them joy.

Name three people you love (e.g., close friends, family members). Beside each name, write out one thing you can do that will bring them happiness this month.

Our obedience pleases God. How will you step out in obedience to God today?

God, thank You for the gift of Jesus, the gift of forgiveness, and the gift of victory through faith. Help me to never take these gifts for granted, but to turn my heart toward You in obedience out of love for You. Thank You for loving me perfectly!

JESUS IS LIFE

discover

READ 1 JOHN 5:5-13.

The one who has the Son has life. The one who does not have the Son of God does not have life.
—1 John 5:12

People who love us sometimes do things that we don't understand but are for our good. Maybe your parents won't allow you to date or have your own phone until a certain age. Maybe your teacher doesn't accept late assignments. Maybe your student pastor says you can't lead a small group of younger kids until you're a senior in high school. These rules might upset you, but they are for your good, and they exist for good reasons. You can choose to obey and be rewarded at the right time or disobey and suffer the consequences of your choices.

Sometimes what we know about the person giving the rule determines our obedience. We know Jesus is who He says He is. In Jesus's day, Jewish law required two or three witnesses to give a testimony before declaring something as true. John said that "there are three that testify [about Jesus]: the Spirit, the water, and the blood" (vv. 7-8). Jesus's identity is confirmed through the testimony of the Spirit and the Father at His baptism (*the water*; see Matt. 3:16-17); His death (*the blood*; see Matt. 27:32-56); and the Holy Spirit's ministry (*the Spirit*; see John 15:26).

The reason for this testimony is that we might trust in Him and have eternal life, which is more than just living forever; it's living forever in the presence of God. However, those who choose not to trust in Him will be eternally separated from Him. Choosing sin leads to death; choosing Jesus is life.

delight

God's own testimony about Jesus should carry the greatest weight. Look at Matthew 3:16-17. Who does God say Jesus is? Why does this matter?

The gift of eternal life isn't so much about living forever as it is about being in relationship with Jesus eternally. How does this affect your perspective on eternal life?

display

God gave testimony about who Jesus is so we could know the truth. We are to also give testimony about who Jesus is so those around us can know the truth and receive the gift of eternal life in Him. The consequences of people not knowing the truth are significant. The gift of knowing the truth is eternal.

Use the space provided to write out your testimony about how Jesus has made you new. Then, commit to sharing this testimony with someone within the next two weeks.

God, thank You for providing eternal life through Jesus and giving us Your testimony and Your Word to show us the truth. Show me how to lovingly share the truth of eternity with those who don't know You. Give me the words to speak, and help me to know the right time.

HEARD & ANSWERED

discover

READ 1 JOHN 5:14-17.

**This is the confidence we have before him: If we ask
anything according to his will, he hears us. And if
we know that he hears whatever we ask, we know
that we have what we have asked of him.
—1 John 5:14-15**

Do you remember hearing your parents talk about the "magic word" when you asked them for something as a kid? This "magic" word, "please," was often the difference between receiving what you asked for and being told "no." Of course, if it wasn't best for you, you'd get that "no" anyway. It wasn't about actually making the request but about asking for the right things, the right way, and from the right heart.

Like your parents, God won't give you everything you ask for. But when we ask for the right things (what honors Him); the right way ("according to His will": being willing to go with "no" if that's what He says); and from the right heart (a request motivated by the desire to love, honor, glorify, and obey Him), we can be confident that He hears us.

While this might seem confusing and maybe a little uncomfortable, the good news is the longer we follow Jesus, the more our hearts become tuned to Him. When that happens, our desires shift toward His. At that point, John says we can be confident that Jesus has heard us and will answer because our hearts have been revealed as aligned with His.

delight

How does it make you feel to know that even if God answers your request with a "no," He has listened to you with compassion and love? Why does it make you feel this way?

Read the following Scriptures and summarize what they teach you about prayer: Mark 11:24; John 14:13-14; 15:16; James 4:3.

display

Making a sincere request doesn't guarantee a "yes" from God. Just because something is good doesn't mean it's best for you or aligned with God's will. Prayer isn't so much about telling God our hearts as it is getting to know His. When you pray, try asking, "God, will you show me your point of view about _____ (situation/person) so that I can know how to pray?"

Search your heart, and using the model above, write out one request. As you continue to pray this way, write what you learn.

Father, will You show me Your heart? Will You show me Your point of view concerning the requests I make? Help me to ask the right things, the right way, and from the right heart, being confident that You will hear and answer.

HONOR & IDOLS

discover

READ 1 JOHN 5:18-21.

Little children, guard yourselves from idols.
—1 John 5:21

In these final verses of John's first letter, he moves from assurance about salvation and answered prayer to making sure his readers have the right understanding of sin, the world, and Jesus. As the entire letter was to serve as a reminder of who (Jesus) and what (the gospel) the people already knew, John started every sentence of this final review with "We know …" We know those who love God don't continue in sin or walk in step with the enemy. We know believers are "of God" and "the whole world" is under the enemy's influence. We know that Jesus—and His gift of the Holy Spirit—helps us know Him and understand God's Word; we are in Him and have the gift of eternal life in His presence. This is what we know so far.

Then John closed the letter out with, "guard yourselves from idols." If this seems abrupt or out of place to you, you're not alone; scholars have often debated the meaning of this verse. But as this passage summarizes the entire letter, many believe the word "idols" points to everything John warned about: hatred, disobedience, jealousy, lies, lust, and false teaching. Basically, John's summary of his first letter was this: Jesus is the one true God. Be satisfied in Him and reject the lies.

delight

Read Matthew 6:19-24; Colossians 2:18; 3:5; and 1 Peter 4:3. What are some idols mentioned in these verses beyond the ones John talked about in today's passage?

Now, read Matthew 6:33; Colossians 3:2; and Philippians 4:8. How can we shift our focus from idols back to Jesus (see also 1 Thess. 1:9)?

display

Although the false teachers might not have been worshiping the idols that were so common in the Roman Empire during those days, in a way, they created an idol of their own: a substitute for the One they denied as the one true God. They put their own desires and opinions above the truth about Jesus. Anything we put before Jesus is an idol—a counterfeit god. What are some things—either good or bad—you are tempted to put before God? Spend some time in prayer, talking with God about these things.

Jesus, forgive me for the times I seek things, pleasures, or people before I seek You and Your kingdom. I know You will take care of all I need; I confess the times I'm tempted to follow gods of my own making. Help me to honor Your rightful place in my life.

UNBLOCKED

Communicating Authentically and Peacefully

John modeled several biblical principles for us that can teach us how to communicate authentically and peacefully with others. Think about a specific situation where you need to communicate honestly and lovingly—and in person. Under each verse, write out how you plan to do that.

Be prepared to give an answer. Know the truth so you can respond in truth. (See 1 Peter 3:15.)

Listen fully and carefully before you respond—if you need to say anything at all. Ask yourself: What is this person really saying? (See James 1:19.)

Season your words with grace. The way you talk to people shows them—and others—who your heart belongs to. (See Col. 4:6.)

Tell the truth, but don't hide behind "I was just being honest" or "Sorry, I'm really blunt." Be kind with the words, tone, and even facial expressions you use. (See Eph. 4:15.)

Choose to live at peace with others. You can't control the way they respond to you, but you can control the message you send; let it be one of peace and Jesus. (See Rom. 12:18.)

2 JOHN

SECTION 2

While John's first letter never specified a recipient, the second letter was written to "the elect lady and her children," which was probably a specific church. This letter contains many of the same themes as 1 John and was likely written around the same time. False teachers were still very much a threat to the young church and might have been attempting to take advantage of this congregation's hospitality.

In this letter, John warned his readers not to welcome those who spread lies; instead, he reminded them once more of true Christian teaching and the importance of remaining steadfast in their faith. He invites us to hear this truth and do the same.

"FROM GOD" THINGS

discover

READ 2 JOHN 1-3.

Grace, mercy, and peace will be with us from God the Father and from Jesus Christ, the Son of the Father, in truth and love.
—2 John 3

When you use someone's quote as a social media post or even to make a point in a paper, you're supposed to give them credit to say, "I agree with and love these ideas, but they didn't originate with me." Even in this devotional, you'll see a list of references at the end that match up with quotes used throughout the book. Doing this communicates a respect for the original author (and keeps you in line with copyright laws!).

As James said, we know every good gift comes from God (see James 1:17). The grace, mercy, peace, love, and truth John mentioned are all good "from God" things. John pointed back to the Source, the Author, and made it clear that the grace, mercy, peace, love, and truth we have is "from God the Father and from Jesus Christ." These are gifts—not things God gives begrudgingly, but freely and authentically.

Rather than sending well-wishes in the greeting of his second letter, John began with assurances. Because of Jesus, John could share confidently that these gifts "will be with us." What better gift to give than a reminder of what God has given us and the reality we now live in? Because we have Him, we will have all the grace, mercy, peace, love, and truth we will ever need.

delight

Out of this authentic love, freely given, we can also freely give grace, mercy, peace, love, and truth to others. Why is this important to the health of the church? Why is it important to the gospel message?

How does this passage encourage you for the times you don't feel capable of being gracious, merciful, peaceful, loving, or truthful?

display

John's use of "in truth and love" reveals the theme of his second letter. Christians should be completely committed to the truth of the gospel and to loving one another sacrificially as Jesus called us to.

Name one way you love other Christians well.

Name one thing you need to work on to love others better.

Heavenly Father, I know every good gift comes from You. Thank You for the gift of Jesus and for the gifts of grace, mercy, peace, love, and truth we have in Him. Please help me to give those same gifts to the people around me.

FORM & FOLLOW-THROUGH

discover

READ 2 JOHN 4-6.

This is love: that we walk according to his commands. This is the command as you have heard it from the beginning: that you walk in love.
—2 John 6

If you've ever played on a basketball team or attended a basketball camp, you've likely heard the acronym *BEEF*: Balance, Elbows, Eyes, Follow-through. This is the four-step process to help you develop the best form for shooting the ball. Here's the breakdown: *Balance* your feet shoulder-width apart. Set the *elbow* of your shooting-arm at a ninety-degree angle and directly under the ball. (Your other hand rests lightly on the side of the ball as nothing more than a guide.) Fix your *eyes* on the basket. *Follow-through* after the shot, straightening your arm with your fingers and wrist pointing down at the court. It's a useful acronym, but just knowing it won't improve your game; you must practice it again and again to build good form.

In his letters, John coaches us on good form for following-through with Jesus. In fact, maybe John's admonition to "walk" could be summed up with the acronym *STROLL*: Study, Truth, Remember, Obedience, Love, Lord. *Study* God's Word. Learn the *truth* and get to know the *Truth* (Jesus). Move forward by *remember*ing what you've learned. Then walk in *obedience* to it. *Love* God and others. And through it all, honor Jesus as *Lord*. As we continue to "develop our form," others will see it as evidence of our faith and the truth about Jesus.

Truth and Love

delight

To walk in love is continuous and general. We are to love everyone always. Why is that be difficult? Who is it difficult to always love?

Using the "*STROLL*" acronym, what is the area in which you need the most work developing your "form" and "follow-through"?

display

Use the *STROLL* acronym to talk about how each word will influence your words and actions this week.

S: How will you study God's Word?

T: What truth have you learned this week from your study?

R: What truth can you remember and apply that you already know?

O: Which step of obedience is God calling you to take?

L: Who is God calling you to reach out to in love? How can you show your love for God?

L: How will you honor Jesus as Lord this week?

God, help me love everyone always—no matter how difficult they might be to get along with. Help me to embrace every part of the gospel message and obey it. May my words and actions lead others to Your truth and love.

MEMORY VERSE

This is love: that we walk according to his commands. This is the command as you have heard it from the beginning: that you walk in love.

—2 John 6

MORE OR LESS

discover

READ 2 JOHN 7-9.

**Anyone who does not remain in Christ's teaching but goes beyond it does not have God. The one who remains in that teaching, this one has both the Father and the Son.
—2 John 9**

By the time Jesus began His public ministry, self-righteousness and cold-hearted religion were everywhere. God had given the Jews ten commandments, and Jesus even simplified them down to two (see Matt. 22:37-40). But a group called the Pharisees—a prominent sect of Jewish religious leaders and lawmakers—had a system of 613 laws in place that had developed over time. The Pharisees had become their own source of wisdom and called it godliness. They gave less and asked for more while Jesus gave everything.

Jesus told the Pharisees, "You know neither me nor my Father" (John 8:19). The truth wasn't in them. They tried to make God fit their mold, their laws, and their culture instead of seeking and obeying His will. John warned his readers about others who might do this to them and about doing this themselves.

While we are to be constantly and diligently learning about Jesus and growing in our faith, we are not to go against or add to what has been taught in God's Word. So, we "remain in Christ's teaching" and keep living out what we learn from Scripture. This is proof that we "have God." Our faith is revealed by what we live.

delight

When have you seen people try to add to the truth of Scripture (i.e., saying the Bible teaches something it doesn't)?

When have you seen people try to go against Scripture (i.e., ignoring what's really in the Bible)?

display

John said "watch yourselves" when it comes to false teaching. John wasn't being sarcastic or snarky; he was pleading for us to diligently defend ourselves against false teachers and teachings. If you want to know whether someone is a false teacher, ask yourself: Does this person walk in love toward God and others? Does this person obey and teach Jesus's teaching? If you want to know if something is a false teaching, ask yourself: Does this teach me to love God and others? Does this line up with God's Word? Turn loose any false teachers or teachings you identify in your life.

Father, please give me the wisdom and discernment to know when someone isn't speaking truth. Help me grow in my knowledge of You and Your Word so I can easily spot false teachings, too. I pray that whatever I say and do lines up with Your Word.

RECEIVE & GREET

discover

READ 2 JOHN 10-13.

**If anyone comes to you and does not bring this teaching,
do not receive him into your home, and do not greet him;
for the one who greets him shares in his evil works.
—2 John 10-11**

As we saw yesterday, those who teach anything other than—either less *or* more than—what Jesus taught don't "have God" (v. 9). In other words, they live according to their own rules and try to teach others that their rules are the right way. Now it seems like John is teaching that believers shouldn't ask these people to hang out or even say "hi" to them. That sounds a little harsh, right? Aren't we supposed to still be gracious, kind, and loving to those who are confused about God?

To understand what John was saying, we must look at the cultural context. Consider how Paul traveled and stayed with people who either wanted to hear his message or had already received it and wanted him to share with others. While Paul worked in his profession as a tentmaker so people wouldn't have to support him everywhere he went, this wasn't the case for everyone. It was normal for believers to offer a place to stay, food, and even financial aid to these missionaries.

This means John wasn't saying not to say "hi" or spend time with someone like this; he was saying not to support the ministry of those who teach anything other than the gospel of Jesus. We should pray for them to see the truth and come to faith, but we shouldn't bless their ministry.

delight

What do you think John meant by saying those who "greet" (affirm) false teachers share in their work?

How might the opposite also be true—those who "greet" (affirm) gospel teachers do share in their work?

display

Although believers are not called to be rude or inconsiderate toward nonbelievers, we are also not supposed to agree with them or affirm their beliefs that are contrary to the teachings of Jesus. Who comes to mind when you think of unbelievers? Use the following chart to record the name of one of these people and note a particular false belief they hold. Then explain how you can encourage them toward Jesus, how you can disagree kindly, and how you can affirm their worth as being made in the image of God without affirming their beliefs.

Name:

False Belief:

Encouragement:

Disagreement:

Affirmation:

Lord Jesus, help me love the lost like You do. Make me bold to speak the truth in love when I know someone is wrong. Help me see how to love unbelievers without affirming or being influenced by their incorrect beliefs. And guide me as I share the gospel with them, too.

3 JOHN

SECTION 3

Although it's tough to pinpoint exactly when this letter was written, it's often called the "twin epistle" to 2 John and was likely written close to the same time as the other two letters. The book of 3 John gets a little more specific in its address, as the recipient is identified in the very first verse as Gaius, a friend of John's in the church.

Though it conveys many of the same ideas as the other letters, this is more personal in tone. The way John spoke about the themes of truth and love are also different, as he chose to use examples of what to do and what not to do in extending hospitality and showing honor to God. In this letter, we see how to apply those examples to our own lives, too.

NO GREATER JOY

discover

READ 3 JOHN 1-4.

**I have no greater joy than this: to hear that
my children are walking in truth.**
—3 John 4

At some point, we've all struggled and had to be taught the right way to do things. Though we'll continue to learn and develop those skills, we can pass along what we've already learned to others. Think about the way you felt when you taught someone how to throw the perfect spiral at football practice. Or maybe when you helped a friend understand a complicated math problem. Or even when you spent extra time going over a song with someone who just joined the band. When they got it, what did you feel? Maybe you'd say it made you happy or you were excited. But maybe you'd call that feeling *joy*.

As one of the original followers who was called to "Go . . . and make disciples" (Matt. 28:19), John knew the meaning of this word well. He knew what it was like to share the gospel and continue discipling—or teaching others to follow God's instructions. As John taught and wrote letters, some believed and some didn't. But for those who did and continued growing in the faith, John expressed deep joy. The word used for *joy* in the Greek, *chara*, indicates a fullness of feeling, an absolute delight.[10]

If all of heaven rejoices when even one sinner repents (see Luke 15:7), so should we. And we should continue that rejoicing every day that they grow closer to the One who saved them.

delight

Even though you are a teenager and still growing in your faith (like everyone else), how can you help disciple others?

How do you respond when you see or hear of someone growing in their faith? After reading this passage, how do you think you are responding well? What, if anything, might need to change about your response?

display

John addressed this letter to a specific disciple, Gaius. Despite the concerns he voiced in these letters, John was always joyful when he greeted his readers. People don't need to be living perfectly in their faith to be "walking in the truth."

Consider one person who might be like John in your life (i.e., someone who disciples and rejoices over you) and one person who might be like Gaius (i.e., someone you disciple and rejoice over). Write each of these people a letter, telling the discipler what their discipleship has meant for your spiritual growth and the disciple how proud of them you are for theirs.

God, thank You for rejoicing over my repentance. Help me to rejoice in the same way when others repent and when they grow in You. Show me the people You want me to disciple and those You want me to be discipled by.

A SAFE PLACE

discover

READ 3 JOHN 5-8.

Dear friend, you are acting faithfully in whatever you do for the brothers and sisters, especially when they are strangers.
—3 John 5

Have you ever taken one of those spiritual gifts inventories? Spiritual gifts are the unique talents, abilities, and callings God has given you so that you may serve Him and others well (see 1 Cor. 12:4-7). Paul talks about these gifts at length in Ephesians 4:11-12 and Romans 12:6-8. While these may not be the exact gifts named on an inventory, they're essentially summarized into categories: leadership, administration, teaching, knowledge, wisdom, prophecy, discernment, exhortation, shepherding, faith, evangelism, apostleship, service/helps, mercy, giving, and hospitality.

We touched on hospitality when we discussed how Christians used to open their homes to missionaries and take care of their needs. Simply put, hospitality is about opening your home and your heart. It's about making room for the lost to hear the gospel and for new believers to learn to walk with Jesus. It's about providing missionaries, pastors, and leaders a place to rest. When you're hospitable, in essence, you create a safe place for others, either physically or spiritually, or both.

John was specifically talking about those traveling and preaching the gospel, though these same truths apply to all believers. We are to care for those who are working for God—however they're doing so—as if we're caring for God (see Matt. 25:40). In this, we partner together to share the gospel for His name's sake and for His glory.

Truth and Love

delight

Would you respond like Gaius if your family were asked to take in a missionary or missionary family? Why or why not?

What do you think it looks like to "send them on their journey in a manner worthy of God"?

display

Hospitality is a huge part of our faith. No matter how old you are, you can practice hospitality toward your brothers and sisters in Christ—whether they're missionaries, pastors, or other Christians seeking to serve the Lord. Using the list on this page, record a few ideas for ways you can show hospitality to people in each group. One idea for each group is provided for you.

Missionaries (e.g., Send a letter of encouragement):

Pastors (e.g., Make cookies or a meal to serve your pastor and family):

Other Christians (e.g., Invite the new student to hang out with you and your friends):

Jesus, help me love Your people like You do. Show me ways I can support and love those who are serving You full-time today as well as other believers who are sharing the gospel in their daily lives. Make me bold to share the gospel, too.

RIGHT WAY/WRONG WAY

discover

READ 3 JOHN 9-10.

I wrote something to the church, but Diotrephes, who loves to have first place among them, does not receive our authority.
—3 John 9

These two verses paint a stark contrast to the person described in verses 1-8, who served and was hospitable to those who came to share the gospel. Unlike Gaius, Diotrephes was not living in obedience to God or to what John had taught. Instead, Diotrephes rebelled against what John taught in three specific ways:

- He wanted to be first and most important in the church.
- He spread gossip about John.
- He refused to receive believers from other churches and even refused to allow those who did into the church.

This is how not to "walk in the truth." If we want to know how to "walk in the truth," we can flip these around to see truths from Gaius's example in the previous passage. This is how Gaius walked in the truth:

- He served and supported others.
- He was faithful to the truth John had taught.
- He welcomed those who came to teach about Jesus "in a manner worthy of God."

Pride, gossip, and unwillingness to love others well often work together to compromise our gospel witness. As believers, everything we do—or don't do—points to Jesus. So, ask yourself, is the portrait of your life painting an accurate picture of who Jesus is and how He loves us?

delight

What did John say Diotrephes loved? What should he have loved most of all instead?

How does John's response to Diotrephes encourage you to respond to people who might say hurtful things about you? Why was it important for John to set the record straight?

display

Examine your heart to see which of these biblical portraits looks most like your life—Gaius or Diotrephes.

Do you want to be in the most important position or the most popular in your youth group?

Do you spread gossip about those in authority over you or those you disagree with?

Do you refuse to serve if a task seems beneath you? Do you refuse to accept other people who serve God, willing to do lowly tasks?

If you answered yes to any of these questions, confess to God any ways you felt convicted and ask Him to help you flip the portrait of your life.

Father, thank You for Your grace and forgiveness. Please help me to never take those for granted by living as if I have a free pass when it comes to sin. May the portrait of my life show others who You really are and bring You glory.

DAY 29

IMITATE GOOD

discover

READ 3 JOHN 11-12.

Everyone speaks well of Demetrius—even the truth itself. And we also speak well of him, and you know that our testimony is true.
—3 John 12

If you ever played a game of "Simon Says" as a kid, you know that if you moved without the leader saying "Simon Says" before the instruction, you were out. The instructions were pretty clear: Move if you hear, "Simon Says." Stay put if you don't hear it. John also gave some clear instructions for who and what those who are "of God" should imitate: do imitate what's good, but don't imitate what's evil. We should carefully consider the people we follow and allow to speak into our lives.

The issue with Diotrephes is sandwiched between two strong examples of those who do good and are of God: Gaius (who we learned about on Days 27–28) and Demetrius (who we'll learn about today). There's only one verse about Demetrius but it tells us a lot about him, and it gives the threefold witness many would have been looking for: all the believers said good things about him, he practiced what he believed and claimed to be true (the gospel), and John and other church leaders testified that he was trustworthy.

People knew who Demetrius was. He was authentic. He lived his faith. He was someone even the apostle John would recommend to his "dear friend" Gaius. For us, even though the description is short, Demetrius is someone worthy of imitating.

delight

Jesus is the ultimate example for believers. How were Gaius and Demetrius imitating Him?

When looking at the examples of Gaius and Demetrius, what are some specific things you can imitate?

display

While the examples John provided are helpful accounts of real people who once lived, they obviously aren't people you can walk with and talk to today. So, review Gaius and Demetrius's characteristics and list the names of people you know who have those same qualities today. Consider meeting consistently with one of these people who can be a mentor in the faith.

Potential mentors:

Thank You, God, for good examples, in both Scripture and in my own life, of people who are consistently walking with You. Please shape me into a person whose life example points back to You in a way that is worthy of being imitated, too.

BE PRESENT

discover

READ 3 JOHN 13-15.

I hope to see you soon, and we will talk face to face.
—3 John 14

It seems like there's a social media platform for every kind of personality. Through various sites, you can post a witty one-liner, photos and videos, or even read those funny posts you know Grandma didn't mean to share. Then, of course, we have texts, video chats, and phone calls. While a shy person might prefer a more behind-the-scenes method of communication like social media, the truth is that we all need real, authentic connections that aren't through a screen.

John didn't always get to communicate in person, either, though he wanted to. While there are benefits to writing a letter, there are downsides, too. For one, John's letter route would've been a lot slower than our post office today. In fact, we know this letter was hand delivered by Demetrius, likely from Ephesus to a smaller church somewhere in Asia Minor. Can you imagine waiting weeks or months for a letter to arrive, especially one about such important issues? This was the world John lived in.

But growing as friends and growing in our faith requires us to be present, physically and mentally. Some things can be described in a letter or digital platform, but John reserved "many things" for in-person communication, and we're wise to do the same.

delight

When John wrote the word "peace" (v. 15), he pointed the readers' attention to God's presence. How can you point others attention to God's presence and peace with your words?

What kinds of things could be difficult for you to talk about face to face? Why might those be the best conversations to have in person?

display

Before you press "send" on your posts this week, use these steps to determine whether what you're putting out there digitally should be said face-to-face or not at all.

For any written/typed words, remember that the recipient can't see your facial expressions or body language, or hear your tone of voice. Ask: How could this be misinterpreted?

For posts made online, remember who's watching you. Ask: Will this be something I want to delete later?

In everything, remember that you represent Jesus. Ask: What does this post/communication tell people about Jesus?

Think about one conversation you really need to have, and make time to have it face to face!

Father, thank You for teaching me to love You and love others well through Your Word. Please help me to live out what I've learned over the last month so others may see Your influence in my life and want to know You, too.

I DID IT FOR LOVE

Look back at the themes of from Day 16 ("Real Love") and use them, along with the questions below, to guide you in writing a journaled prayer. If one of the questions below points to something you haven't yet experienced, think about what you might need from God if you do experience this in the future. Grab a blank sheet of paper, a journal, or even a cheap composition notebook, and write out your prayer.

What have you done and what would you do for love of God and others?

How is God's love changing you?

Heavenly Father, thank You for the ways you've helped me grow in . . .

What sorrows have you endured because of love for God or others?

Jesus, thank You for enduring my sin and the cross because of Your love for me. Thank You for strengthening me to endure, even with (name of situation or person) . . .

What have you given up for love of God and others?

God, I confess I still miss (the thing you gave up) _____.
When You call me to give up something that doesn't honor You or hurts
someone else, please soften my heart to do it willingly.

How does God's love empower you to persevere or forgive when love isn't easy?

You are so merciful and gracious with me, Father. You are patient and
forgiving when I mess up. Help me to imitate Your mercy, grace, patience,
and forgiveness when . . .

What path has God called you to take out of love for Him and others?

Father, I realize You have called me to a completely different way of living.
Specifically, You have called me to love You by . . .

And You have called me to love others by . . .

Help me to hold on to truth and love.

SOURCE

1. "How Eyes See at Night," CooperVision, October 14, 2014, https://coopervision.com/blog/how-eyes-see-night.

2. Robert W. Yarbrough, "1 John," in *CSB Study Bible: Notes*, ed. Edwin A. Blum and Trevin Wax (Nashville, TN: Holman Bible Publishers, 2017), 1994.

3. Daniel L. Akin, "1 John," in *The Apologetics Study Bible: Notes*, Ted Cabal, Chad Brand, E. Ray Clendenen, Paul Copan, and J. P. Moreland, eds., (Nashville, TN: Holman Bible Publishers, 2017), 1559.

4. Bede, "1 John 2:16," in *Ancient Faith Study Bible: Notes*, James Stuart Bell, ed., (Nashville, TN: Holman Bible Publishers, 2019), 1565.

5. Daniel L. Akin, *1, 2, 3 John, vol. 38, The New American Commentary* (Nashville: Broadman & Holman Publishers, 2001), 138.

6. Bede, "1 John 3:18-19," in *Ancient Faith Study Bible: Notes* (Nashville, TN: Holman Bible Publishers, 2019), 1567.

7. Charles H. Spurgeon, "1 John 4:10," in *The Spurgeon Study Bible* (Nashville, TN: Holman Bible Publishers, 2017), 1683.

8. "Love," *Merriam-Webster*, accessed February 8, 2022, https://www.merriam-webster.com/dictionary/love.

9. "Pharisaic Laws," Bible.org, accessed February 9, 2022, https://bible.org/illustration/pharisaic-laws. Outlined from Joseph Stowell, *Fan the Flame* (Chicago: Moody, 1986), 52.

10. "5479. Chara," Bible Hub, accessed August 23, 2022, https://biblehub.com/greek/5479.htm.

☐ JESUS 101

☐ FUELED

☐ ALREADY BUT NOT YET

☐ THE ESSENTIALS

☐ CALLED

☐ PRESENCE & PURPOSE

☐ REVEALED

☐ LION OF JUDAH

☐ YOUR WILL BE DONE

☐ SPIRIT & TRUTH

☐ THREE-IN-ONE

☐ IN THE BEGINNING